KU-111-194

F. WETHERMAN & CO., LTD.,
ENFIELD.

Notes
on the
Cathedrals

LONDON: SWAN SONNENSCHEIN & CO., Lim.

IONA.

Only two great English cathedrals—Salisbury and St. Paul's—stand to-day as their builders left them. The others have been altered; some indeed entirely rebuilt. Of nearly all, the history begins in Saxon times, and may be traced to the buildings which arose as Christianity spread through the Heptarchy. The churches were as a rule but small, possibly no larger than, and of similar style to, the remaining one of Bradford-on-Avon. They were sometimes placed upon sites where Roman temples had stood, the very temple itself in at least one instance — Canterbury — being adapted for Christian worship. With the growth of Norman influence in the country, the scale and magnificence of the buildings increased, and the period closes not unworthily with Waltham Abbey. But it was the Conquest, with the introduction of foreign prelates to the English sees, that may be said to have inaugurated that great building age which, with four principal periods of style that we call Norman, Early English, Decorated, and Perpendicular, lasted for five hundred years. In some of the cathedrals every style can be seen, and it is in tracing the changes that many find their chief, sometimes their only pleasure in the buildings. This, the architectural side of the subject, is

CHURCH OF ST. LAURENCE, BRADFORD-ON-AVON.

of course of supreme importance, but there is something more:

> *As the true disciple gazes, spirit answers spirit, the glorious poem languaged in the stone breaks forth into a silent chant of life, voiceless thoughts breathed out of the fair structure pass into the gazer's soul and enter there, and these revive the memory of noble minds, that built their hearts, their blood, their all, into those walls.*" (*Thring*).

The object, then, of these "Notes" is not merely to give tables of building dates, but also to show how closely the cathedrals are knit to the general history of the land. The lives of the bishops, many of them the leading statesmen of their day, are full of interest, and their monuments, together with those of others not less worthy, arrest attention with an endless variety of story. We stand at the shrine of St. Alban, as thousands of pilgrims have stood before, and the early history of Christianity in Britain is recalled. Not that we are quite at the beginning, for Chichester, with its interesting legend of Pudens and Claudia, carries us back to a still earlier time. But both remind us that the Christian religion came to our country with the Romans. At Durham, the name of Cuthbert is romantically linked with thoughts of Iona, the Celtic missions, and the coming of the Danes. Canterbury tells of Augustine, of the Norman Conquest, of the establishment of foreign prelates in England, and the subsequent contests between the secular powers and the Church, of Chaucer and his Pilgrims. And so we might go on, associating different periods of history with different cathedrals: Salisbury, and Lichfield, and York with the great building age; Winchester with the growth of public schools, and the Universities; Gloucester with the martyrs; Worcester with Cromwell; St. Paul's, and Wakefield with modern times. It would perhaps be best to link Liverpool with the future. For Liverpool is a diocese waiting for its faithful, and its rich, to endow it with a cathedral worthy of themselves, of their great city, and of the Church. But although periods or epochs of history be named with particular cathedrals, it must be remembered that each one can tell nearly the whole history of England in some way. At St. Albans for instance, just as the very stones speak of every date from Roman times to that of the modern restorer, so its associations take us back to the earliest period in the history of our country, and carry us along, through the Conquest, the Middle Ages, the story of Becket, the Peasant Rising, the Wars of the Roses, the Reformation, to the transformation of the old monastic church into the cathedral of to-day.

It may not be out of place here to make a suggestion to the younger readers of this note book who would like to study the history of the cathedrals on the lines that have been indicated. Take a small book, such as Curtis's "Outlines of English History," and re-bind it with interleaves of plain paper. On the plain pages write a list of contemporary work, events, or names in connection with the cathedrals. Several columns should be made and then there will be room for chronological notes of any particular study or "fads" of the compiler. If his taste is for literature, he will note the dates of the appearance of the great authors or their works, he will identify Shakespeare's bishops, and probably find room for a line to mention the monument of Hugh Conway in Bristol Cathedral, commemorating the author of a once very popular book. He will also see the tremendous effect the introduction of printing had on Cathedral building. Or is the study the Prayer Book? Then an entry will be made of the tomb at Ely of Dr. Gunning, the author of the prayer "for all sorts and conditions of men." Bath will furnish matter to those interested in missions in the monument of Dr. Haweis, one of the founders of the London Missionary Society. Is the reader a London man? Then he will be interested in noting that when Whittington was Lord Mayor for the third time the steeple of Old St. Paul's was under repair after damage by lightning. Or does he smoke? He will find on the page of his note book that there was nothing but destruction going on at the cathedrals at the time of the introduction of tobacco! Or is he a politician? If he is, then he will thank Mr. William Watson for his beautiful lines:

. . . . *I count him wise,*
Who loves so well Man's noble memories
He needs must love man's nobler hopes yet more.

TRIFORIUM, ST ALBANS.   SAXON BALUSTERS.

STYLES OF ARCHITECTURE.

ROMAN, BRITISH, SAXON.
NORMAN 1060-1145.
TRANSITIONAL 1145-1190.
EARLY ENGLISH 1190-1272.
DECORATED 1272-1377.
PERPENDICULAR 1377-1547.

The Styles were not divided by a sharp line; between each there was a period of transition, the changes following each other almost as imperceptibly as the seasons of the year. On the next page a more detailed table is adopted.

———

The oldest cathedral building is the crypt of Ripon c.670; St. Albans nave and transept were begun 1077.

The largest cathedral is York; the smallest Wakefield, but Oxford is only fractionally larger. The longest is Winchester, 556 feet, the shortest Oxford 175 feet.

Highest spire, Salisbury, 404 feet; the cross of St. Paul's is 365 feet.

Greatest height of floor above sea level, St. Albans.

ARCHITECTURAL PERIODS.

NORMAN
1060-1145.

WILLIAM I 1066-1087.
Conquest of England.
Domesday Book completed 1086.
WILLIAM II 1087-1100.
Anselm, Archbishop.
HENRY I 1100-1135.
Wreck of the White Ship 1120.
STEPHEN 1135-1154.

TRANSITIONAL
1145-1190.

Battle of the Standard 1138.
Treaty of Wallingford 1153.
HENRY II 1154-1189.
Constitutions of Clarendon 1164.
Murder of Becket 1170.

LANCET
1190-1245.

RICHARD I 1189-1199.
Richard's Crusades 1190-1194
JOHN 1199-1216
England under an Interdict 1208.
Magna Charta 1215.
HENRY III 1216-1272.

GEOMETRICAL
1245-1315.

Friars arrive in England 1220.
The Provisions of Oxford 1258.
Battle of Evesham 1265.
EDWARD I 1272-1307.
Conquest of Scotland 1296.
EDWARD II 1307-1327.

CURVILINEAR
1315-1360.

Battle of Bannockburn 1314.
EDWARD III 1327-1377.
The Black Death 1349.
Battle of Poitiers 1356.

RECTILINEAR
1360-1485.

Wycliffe flourishes at Oxford 1360.
RICHARD II 1377-1399.
The Peasant Revolt 1381.
HENRY IV 1399-1413.
Battle of Shrewsbury 1403.
HENRY V 1413-1422.
Battle of Agincourt 1415.
HENRY VI 1422-1461.
Seige of Orleans 1429.
First Battle of St. Albans 1455.
Battle of Towton 1461.
EDWARD IV 1461-1483.
Battle of Barnet 1471.
Caxton settles in England 1474.
EDWARD V 1483.
RICHARD III 1483-1485.

TUDOR **1485-1547.**	HENRY VII 1485-1509. Colet and Erasmus at Oxford 1499. HENRY VIII 1509-1547. Luther burns the Pope's Bull 1520. Tyndale trans. the New Testt. 1525. Fall of Wolsey 1529. Suppression of Greater Abbeys 1539.
RENAISSANCE **First Period** **1547-1620.**	EDWARD VI 1547-1553. First Prayer Book of Edward VI 1549. MARY 1553-1558. Cranmer burnt at Oxford 1556. ELIZABETH 1558-1603. Mary Stuart executed 1587. Defeat of the Armada 1588. JAMES I 1603-1625. Authorized version of Bible pub. 1611.
Second Period **1620-1702.**	CHARLES I 1625-1649. Battle of Naseby 1645. COMMONWEALTH 1649-1660. Battle of Worcester 1651. Death of Cromwell 1658. CHARLES II 1660-1685. Corporation Act 1661. Act of Uniformity 1662. Fire of London 1666. The Test Act 1673. JAMES II 1685-1688. Trial of the Seven Bishops. WILLIAM III and MARY 1689-1694. WILLIAM alone 1694-1702. Massacre of Glencoe 1692. Peace of Ryswick 1697.
Third Period **1702-1800.**	ANNE 1702-1714. Battle of Blenheim 1704. Trial of Dr. Sacheverel 1710. GEORGE I 1714-1727. The South Sea Bubble 1720. GEORGE II 1727-1760. Battle of Culloden 1746. GEORGE III 1760-1820. Declaration of Independence 1776.
THE GOTHIC **REVIVAL.**	Battle of Waterloo 1815. GEORGE IV 1820-1830. Catholic Emancipation Act 1828 WILLIAM IV 1830-1837. The Reform Act 1832. VICTORIA 1837-1901. EDWARD VII 1901.

CHRONOLOGICAL OUTLINE

OF

THE FOUNDATION OF THE SEES UNDER PRESENT DESIGNATIONS.

Changes of area are ignored.)

447.	SODOR & MAN.	1075.	CHICHESTER.
500.	LLANDAFF.		680.c. Selsey.
516.	BANGOR.	1091.	NORWICH.
522.	ST. DAVID'S.		630. Dunwich.
560.	ST. ASAPH.		674. Elmham.
597.	CANTERBURY.		1070. Thetford.
604.	LONDON.	1109.	ELY.
604.	ROCHESTER.	1133.	CARLISLE.
625.	YORK.	1218.	BATH & WELLS.
669.	LICHFIELD.		904.c. Wells.
	1075. Chester.		1092.c. Bath.
	1096.c. Coventry	1220.	SALISBURY.
	1183. Coventry & Lichfield.		705. Sherborne.
			909. Wilton.
	1661. Lichfield & Coventry.		1075. Old Sarum.
		1541.	CHESTER.
	1836. Lichfield.	1541.	GLOUCESTER.
676.	HEREFORD.	1541.	PETERBORO'
679.	WINCHESTER.	1545.	OXFORD.
	635. Dorchester		1542. Osney.
680.	WORCESTER.	1836.	RIPON.
995.	DURHAM.	1847.	MANCHESTER.
	635. Lindisfarne.	1877.	TRURO.
	883. Chester-le-Street.	1878.	ST. ALBANS.
		1880.	LIVERPOOL.
1050.	EXETER.	1882.	NEWCASTLE.
	909.c. Crediton.	1884.	SOUTHWELL.
1071.	LINCOLN.	1888.	WAKEFIELD.
	678. Lindsey.	1897.	BRISTOL.
	680. Leicester.		1542. Bristol.
	870. Dorchester.		1836. Gloucester & Bristol.

THE DIOCESES
CATHEDRAL CITIES
and Counties of
ENGLAND & WALES

Scale
0   20   40   60   80
English Miles
Cathedral Cities.....+

CANTERBURY.

THE CATHEDRAL FROM THE SOUTH-WEST

In 1070 the Norman Lanfranc was consecrated Archbishop, and commenced to rebuild the Cathedral. On a subsequent page the various building dates are given, but it may now be said that Canterbury does not owe its chief interest to its architectural story and features, but to its great names, and to its close association with the history of England. In historic interest it has but one rival—St. Albans, but in its association with famous Englishmen it is easily first. What thrilling scenes are recalled by the mention of only a few of the names: Augustine, Alphege, Anselm, Langton, the Black Prince, Cranmer and Laud! But one name stands out clear of all others. It is of Thomas Becket that we think when we visit Canterbury. All interest centres in him, and gathers round the stirring story of his life.

The picture of King Henry II doing penance at Becket's tomb recalls to our mind the power of the Church and great churchmen in Mediæval times. Archbishops and Bishops must join the Crusades ; the Barons need Stephen Langton to lead them against King John; Archbishop Edmund Rich (St. Edmund) is found on the popular side in the disturbances of Henry III's reign—he now has his fitting reward, a place in the beautiful window of the Chapter House. By way of contrast we see Simon of Sudbury instigating the Poll Tax which led to the Peasant Revolt, and he is beheaded by the followers of Wat Tyler. And so the story goes on, nearly all the leading events of English History finding some association with the Cathedral.

Features to be Noticed.

Existing Cathedral covers, as nearly as can be ascertained, the same ground as the original building of Lanfranc, with exception of the retro-choir or extreme eastern part, which is much longer.

Gradual ascent from W. porch to place of High Altar.

Approach of walls to each other at eastern end of choir.

Choir longest in England—180 feet.

Choir earliest specimen of "Transitional."

Work of nave to be compared with that of William of Wykeham (seven years earlier) at Winchester.

Piers of central tower buttressed: to be compared with buttressing at Wells, Salisbury, and Westminster Abbey.

Curious position of Stephen Langton's coffin in Warrior chapel.

The ancient stained glass in Trinity chapel.

Chair of St. Augustine.

BUILDING DATES.

1070. Cathedral and Monastery entirely rebuilt by Lanfranc; work completed 1077. Now existing, foundations of nave, and W. towers, portions of W. transept walls, core of piers of central tower, and parts of crypt, and monastery.
1096. Choir begun by Prior Ernulph.
1130. Choir completed : the "Glorious Choir of Conrad." Now remaining, two chapels, crypt, and other portions.
1174. The "Glorious Choir" burnt.
      Present choir begun by William of Sens.
1178. Work continued by William the Englishman.
1184. Choir completed.
1190. Cloisters begun.
1220. The Corona consecrated.
1304. Screen work of Prior d'Estria begun. Completed c.1305. Chapter House begun.
1336. South window in Anselm's tower inserted by Prior d'.Estria.
1363. Black Prince's chantry in crypt.
1378. Nave Lanfranc's) pulled down by Abp. Sudbury. Present nave begun by Prior Chillenden. Chapter House completed. Cloisters completed.
1400.c. Spire to NW. tower (destroyed 1834) ; South Porch ; Warrior Chapel ; Peal of five bells.
1443. Chantry of Henry IV.
1449. The Deans Chapel built by Prior Goldstone I.
1450.c. Western screen of choir.
1465. Window of N. transept presented by Edward IV. and his Queen.
1495. Buttressing-arches to tower piers, and upper part of Angel tower built by Prior Goldstone II.
1507. Christ Church gateway begun by Prior Goldstone II. Completed 1517.
1642. Puritans destroy reredos, and other features.
1702. Old stalls removed by Abp. Tenison, and pews substituted, Prior d'Estria's screen concealed with wainscoating, new return stalls with canopies erected at W end of choir. All altered 1877.
1704. Throne (since replaced) carved by Grinling Gibbons.
1828. Tenison's wainscoating removed, and new throne erected.
1834. NW. tower.
1872. Part of roof burnt September 3rd.
1877. Sir Gilbert Scott's restorations begun.

MONUMENTS.

In addition to those mentioned under "Historical Notes," there are monuments, or tombs of Edward the Black Prince (died 1376), Henry IV (1413), Margaret Holland (1437) and her two husbands, the Earl of Somerset and the Duke of Clarence; Coligny, brother of Admiral Coligny; Nicholas Wotton (1567), the first Dean of Canterbury; Dean Boys (1625); Orlando Gibbons (1625), organist of Charles II; Meric Casaubon (1671), son of Isaac Casaubon; Dean Turner (1672), the faithful friend of Charles I; Sir George Rooke (1709), who won the battle of La Hogue, and who took Gibraltar; with others of less interest.

There are also memorial windows to Dean Alford (1871) and Dean Stanley.

DIMENSIONS OF CATHEDRAL.

Total length 522 feet. Choir 180 feet. Breadth of nave and aisles 71 feet. Central tower 235 feet. W. towers 130 feet.

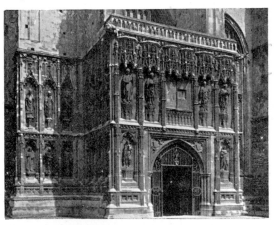

SOUTH-WEST PORCH.

THE NAVE

THE CHOIR.

THE BLACK PRINCE'S TOMB.

THE CORONA.

THE MARTYRDOM.

STEPHEN LANGTON'S TOMB.

ARCHBISHOP CHICHELE'S MONUMENT.

Historical Notes.

Archbishops' names are in heavy letter.   Monuments are noted *.

A.D.

43-410.   ROMAN OCCUPATION OF BRITAIN.
            First introduction of Christianity.

449.   ENGLISH LAND IN BRITAIN.

457.   Kent conquered by English.
         Disappearance of Christianity.

597.   Augustine lands in Kent.
         Augustine : first Archbishop of Canterbury.

655.   **Deus-Dedit** : the first Saxon Archbishop.

668.   **Theodore** : possibly originated the diocesan
            division of England.

741.   **Cuthbert** :   said   to   have   caused   the   Lord's
            Prayer and Creed to be taught in the vulgar tongue.

787.   DANES FIRST LAND IN ENGLAND.

890.   **Plegmund** : before his elevation, King Alfred's
            tutor.

942.   **Odo** : "The Severe," a warlike Dane, and Church
            reformer.

960.   **Dunstan** : some time Abbot of Glastonbury.

1005.   **Alphege** : murdered by the Danes, 1011

1052. **Stigand** : last Saxon Archbishop ; deposed 1070.
1066. NORMAN CONQUEST OF ENGLAND.
1070. **Lanfranc** : first Norman Archbishop ; rebuilt Cathedral.
1093. **Anselm** : outlawed by Rufus 1095 ; goes to Rome 1097 ; recalled by Henry I 1100 ; died 1109.
*1162. **Thomas Becket** : quarrels with Henry II at Woodstock 1163 ; flies to France 1164 ; murdered 1170 ; canonized 1173.
1174. Henry II does penance at Becket's tomb.
1185. **Baldwin** : a Crusader, died at Acre.
1193. **Hubert Fitz Walter** : a Crusader, an admirable Chancellor.
*1207. **Stephen Langton** : leads the Barons in compelling John to grant the Great Charter.
1220. TRANSLATION OF BECKET'S REMAINS. The Friars arrive in England.
1234. **Edmund Rich** : sides with National Party against Henry III ; canonized 1246.
*1279. **John Peckham** : first bishop to enter Parliament.
1279. Statute of Mortmain.
*1294. **Robert Winchelsea** : withstood Edward I's exactions, and excommunicated Gaveston.
*1313. **Walter Reynolds** : before his elevation, tutor, and Chancellor of Edward II.
*1328. **Simon Mepham** : refused admission to Exeter Cathedral by Bishop Grandisson.
*1333. **John Stratford** : opposed the French wars of Edward III ; founded a collegiate church at Stratford-on Avon.
*1349. **Thomas Bradwardine** : author of a great work defending Augustinian doctrines of grace ; died of the plague a few months after consecration. Three Archbishops, Ufford, Bradwardine, and Islip were consecrated in 1349.
1364.c. *Chaucer's Canterbury Tales written, printed about 1475.*
*1375. **Simon Sudbury** : proposer of the Poll Tax ; imprisoned John Ball ; beheaded during Wat Tyler's rebellion.
*1381. **William Courtenay** : when Bishop of London, tried Wycliffe.
1397. **Thomas Arundel** : a cruel persecutor of the Lollards ; exiled 1398, restored 1399.
*1414. **Henry Chichele** : founded All Souls College, Oxford, in remorse for his instigation of Henry V's French war. The Fellows of the College keep his tomb in repair.
*1452. **John Kemp** : present at the battle of Agincourt.

*1454. **Thomas Bourchier**: patron of education and printing; married Henry VII to Elizabeth of York.

1474. CAXTON SETTLES IN ENGLAND.

*1486. **John Morton**: author of "Morton's Fork."

*1503. **William Warham**: "the precursor of the Reformation"; friend of Erasmus.

1512. Dean Colet and Erasmus visit Canterbury.

1516. *More's Utopia written; translation 1551.*

1525. TYNDALE TRANSLATES THE NEW TESTT.

1533. **Thomas Cranmer**: first Protestant Archbishop.

1538. Becket's Shrine stripped.

1539. SUPPRESSION OF THE GREATER ABBEYS, including Christ Church and St. Augustine's, Canterbury.

1556. Cranmer burnt at Oxford.

*1556. **Reginald Pole**: the last Archbishop of Canterbury to acknowledge Papal Supremacy, and the last to be interred in the Cathedral until Archbishop Benson.

1559. **Matthew Parker**: Queen Elizabeth's first Archbishop.

1561. Crypt of Cathedral assigned to French Protestants.

1583. **John Whitgift**: persecutor of the Puritans; founded school and hospital at Croydon.

1604. **Richard Bancroft**: a persecutor of the Puritans; superintended Authorized Version of the Bible.

1633. **William Laud**: imprisoned 1640; beheaded 1645. See vacant for sixteen years.

1660. **William Juxon**: when Bishop of London, attended Charles I at his execution.

1663. **Gilbert Sheldon**: builder of the Sheldonian Theatre at Oxford.

1678. **William Sancroft**: tried as one of the Seven Bishops 1688; deprived 1690 for refusing oath of allegiance to William and Mary.

1691. **John Tillotson**: one of the finest preachers of his time.

1695. **Thomas Tenison**: a famous preacher; founder of free school at St. Martin's-in-the-Fields, London.

1738. THE METHODISTS APPEAR IN KENT.

*1828. **William Howley**: crowns the Queen 1837.

1846. *Railway from London to Canterbury completed.*

*1848. **John Bird Sumner.**

*1868. **Archibald Campbell Tait.**

*1882. **Edward White Benson.**

1896. **Frederick Temple.**

THE CRYPT

NORMAN STAIRCASE IN THE CLOSE.

ST. PAUL'S.

THE CATHEDRAL FROM THE SOUTH-EAST.

WE do injustice to St. Paul's if we connect its history only with the present building. The Cathedral that we know to-day is little more than two hundred years old; but it is the third, possibly the fourth church that has occupied the present site, and a temple to Diana probably preceded the churches. Of Christianity in Roman Londinium we know little. A British bishop, Restitutus, is said to have been present at the Council of Arles in 314, and he may have been Bishop of London. It is a pleasing tradition anyhow, and one which we need not lightly set aside. In Saxon times we get on surer ground. Augustine consecrated Millitus Bishop in 604, and he, with the aid of Ethelbert, King of Kent, built the first St. Paul's, which was endowed with the manor of Tillingham, in Essex, an endowment retained to-day by the Dean and Chapter. This church, in which Kings Edmund and Canute were crowned, was burnt, and probably entirely rebuilt in 962, but again burnt down in 1087. Before this, however, the first Synod of the English Church was held within its walls. In 1087 was begun, by Bishop Mauritius, the church that is known to history as "Old St. Paul's." When completed, the Cathedral was the finest in England. Its history carries with it the history of the great city. It was the church of Whittington; Sir Thomas More and Erasmus knew it, while Colet was one of its famous deans. There, was the noted "Paul's Walk," and the crypt, used after

THE WEST FRONT.

1256, as the parish church of St. Faith's, was the scene of the tragedy of Ainsworth's novel. The famous outdoor pulpit, Paul's Cross, was on the north-east. The Cathedral was subject to the usual routine of Mediæval alteration and rebuilding. Classic additions had been made, and others were in contemplation, when the Great Fire put an end to it all.

What a blessing that fire was to those who love their London. How miserably out of place to-day would be Old St. Paul's. What a crowning glory to the mighty city is the present Cathedral! Not only is it one of the most wonderful and beautiful things in architecture, but it speaks to us of the greater liberty of life and thought brought about by the Renaissance. Dr., afterwards Sir Christopher Wren was appointed principal architect for the rebuilding of London, and of St. Paul's. In 1670 all attempts at restoring the old Cathedral were abandoned, and plans were prepared for an entirely new building. The progress was remarkable, the choir being opened on Dec. 2nd, 1697, with a thanksgiving service for the Peace of Ryswick, and with the completion of the dome in 1710 the work was done. It was a great triumph, the work of one architect, one master-mason (Strong), and completed during the rule of one bishop. Portland stone was used; the iron-work was from the, now extinct, furnaces of the Sussex Weald. The first monument, John Howard's, was erected in 1790, and it has been followed by, on the whole, a most excellent series, commemorative (sometimes with extravagant epitaph) of some very great names in British history. On the wall above Wren's tomb in the crypt, and above the door of the north transept is the famous inscription: *Lector, si Monumentum requiris circumspice.*

❧ ❧ ❧

FEATURES TO BE NOTICED.

The general magnificence of the whole building; the most important Renaissance Church in England. Construction of the building generally, but especially of the double dome and lantern. The apparent difference in the height of interior and exterior walls; as seen from exterior the upper order is simply a screen to hide the flying buttresses. Projection of nave walls at W. end, forming on W. the Morning Chapel, and on S. the Consistory Court—features on the architectural merits of which much has been written for and against. Wood carving of Grinling Gibbons. Sir W. Richmond's mosaics and windows.

Building Dates.

607.c. First Cathedral built by Ethelbert, King of Kent, probably burnt down and rebuilt in 962.

1087.c. Cathedral destroyed by fire. The second Cathedral, "Old St. Paul's" begun.

1136.(?)Fire damaged, possibly destroyed, the building.

1221. Choir rebuilt.

1225. Lady Chapel built.

1240. Consecration of the Church. When c mpleted, the total length of the Cathedral is said to have been 620 feet; height of nave roof 130 feet; of choir 101 feet.

1312. Nave paved with marble.

1315. The Spire rebuilt in wood, covered with lead; height over 460 feet, the then highest in the world.

1422.c. Paul's Cross erected by Cardinal Kemp.

1444. Spire damaged by lightning; repaired c. 1462.

1561. Spire destroyed by lightning, and not rebuilt.

1631.c. Inigo Jones built the Classic west front.

1643. Paul's Cross destroyed by Lord Mayor Penington.

1663. Christopher Wren appointed surveyor.

1666. The Cathedral destroyed in the Great Fire.
A few fragments of "Old St. Paul's" are to be found in the Churchyard.

1674. Ruins of old church began to be removed.

1675. First stone of new building laid June 21st.

1697. Choir opened for service, Dec. 2nd.

1710. The Dome completed.
The total cost of the building was about £1,000,000, the greater part of which was raised by coal and wine dues.

1718. Wren dismissed from office.

1795. First monument (Howard) erected.

1822. Ball and cross restored.

1858-60. Choir screen removed and re-erected at N. door. Organ placed above stalls on N. side. Other changes in arrangement of choir.

1864. Internal decorations continued.

1870. Choir floor raised; organ divided into two parts and placed at W. end of choir; other changes in arrangement of choir.

1872. "Thanksgiving Fund" established.

1874. Iron railing removed from W. front.

1878. Peal of bells; "Great Paul" 1882.

1886. New statue of Queen Anne uncovered.

1888. Reredos completed.

1891. Sir W. Richmond's work begun.

1892. Wellington monument removed to nave.

MONUMENTS.

In Old St. Paul's the following were buried: Sebba, King of the East Saxons; Archbishop Alphege, Ethelred the Unready; John of Gaunt, Dean Colet, Philip Sidney, Francis Walsingham. Portions of six monuments from Old St. Paul's remain, including those of Dr. Donne (1631), Dean of St. Paul's; Sir Nicholas Bacon (1579), father of Lord Bacon; Lord Chancellor Hatton (1591), one of the judges of Mary Stuart, after whom Hatton Garden is named.

The first monument to be erected in the new Cathedral was to John Howard the philanthropist (1790). The second was to Dr. Johnson (1794). In corresponding angles are Sir Joshua Reynolds (1792), and Sir William Jones the Orientalist (1794). Among other important and interesting monuments are those to Wellington (1852); General Gordon (1885); General Herbert Stewart (1885); Lord Melbourne (1848); Admiral Duncan (1804); General Picton (1815), General Napier, historian (1860); Henry Hallam, historian (1859); Nelson (1805); Sir Ralph Abercromby (1801); Sir John Moore (1809); Turner, greatest of painters (1861); Admiral Collingwood, of Trafalgar (1810); General Cornwallis of Yorktown and India (1805); Dean Milman (1868); Bishop Heber (1826); Canon Liddon (1890); Lord Leighton (1896); Sir John Millais (1896); Sir John Goss (1880); Sir E. Landseer (1873); Benjamin West (1820).

THE FONT.

THE CHOIR.

THE NAVE LOOKING WEST.

THE NELSON MONUMENT.

THE WELLINGTON MONUMENT.

THE SOUTH CHOIR AISLE.

THE BISHOP'S THRONE AND STALL.

GENERAL GORDON'S MONUMENT.

Historical Notes.

Bishops' names are in heavy letter.

A.D.

43-410. ROMAN OCCUPATION OF BRITAIN.
First introduction of Christianity.
459. ENGLISH LAND IN BRITAIN.
477. London taken by English.
597. Augustine lands in Kent.
604. **Millitus**: first Bishop of London; in 619, Archbishop of Canterbury.
654. **Cedd**; brother of St. Chad of Lichfield; first
bishop after 30 years of heathenism.
675. **Erkenwald**: great benefactor of the Cathedral;
he was canonized, and his shrine was a place of
worship until the Reformation.
787. DANES FIRST LAND IN ENGLAND.
958. **Dunstan**: sometime Abbot of Glastonbury.
1051. **William the Norman**: Chaplain of Edward
the Confessor; his influence with the Conqueror
obtained restoration of privileges to citizens of the
City; in grateful remembrance an annual pilgrimage was made to his tomb for at least 500 years.

1066. NORMAN CONQUEST OF ENGLAND.

1086. **Mauritius**: Chaplain and Chancellor of Conqueror.

1108. **Richard de Belmeis**: endeavoured, unsuccessfully, to make London an archbishopric.

1163. **Gilbert Foliot**: Pope Alexander promoted him for his ability, to rule over the City that "is more noble and famous than all other cities of the world;" opposed Becket, excommunicated by him.

1199. **William de Sancta Maria**: read Papal interdict of England; subsequently, with Langton, received King John's submission.

1263. **Henry de Sandwich**: a leader on side of Simon de Montfort; excommunicated by the Pope; six years in Rome obtaining pardon.

1280. **Richard de Gravesend**: resisted demands of Edward I. for taxation of clergy.

1319. **Stephen de Gravesend**: nephew of Bishop Richard; resisted visitation of Archbishop of Canterbury; disputed deposition of Edward II.

1362. **Simon Sudbury**: translated to Canterbury; beheaded during Wat Tyler's rebellion.

1375. **William Courtnay**: tried John Wycliff.

1382. **Robert de Braybroke**: honoured by the City for making peace with the King after refusal of loan; vigorous advocate of Sunday observance.

1397. Whittington Lord Mayor, also in 1406 and 1419.

1405. **Roger de Walden**: in absence of Arundel, Archbishop of Canterbury; subsequently Bishop of London; buried in St. Bartholomew's.

1407. **Robert Clifford**: present at Council of Constance; introduced the Use of Sarum to Cathedral.

1450. **Thomas Kemp**: Bishop for 39 years—the whole period of the Wars of the Roses; built the Divinity Schools at Oxford.

1474. CAXTON SETTLES IN ENGLAND.

1502. **William Warham**: "the precursor of the Reformation"; friend of Erasmus.

1512. St. Paul's School founded by Dean Colet.

1516. *More's Utopia written; translation* 1551.

1525. TYNDALE TRANSLATES THE NEW TEST.

1540. **Edmund Bonner**: imprisoned in the Tower under Edward VI; restored by Mary; deprived by Elizabeth, and imprisoned in the Marshalsea, where he died 1569.

1550. **Nicholas Ridley**: introduced the new service book, the present liturgy, to the Cathedral; his influence led to foundation of Christ's Hospital; burnt at Oxford 1555.

1559. **Edmund Grindall** : a gentle and pious guide in troubled times.
1560. Alex. Nowell, dean ; author of first part of Catechism.
1570. **Edwin Sandys** : advised execn. of Mary Stuart.
1572. Massacre of St. Bartholemew.
1577. **John Alymer** : tutor to Lady Jane Grey, a persecutor of Catholics *and* Puritans.
1595. **Richard Fletcher** : incurred wrath of Elizabeth by second marriage.
1602. John Overall, dean ; author of latter part of Catechism.
1611. **John King** : the last of two Bishops of Church of England (Lichfield the other) to burn heretics.
1628. **William Laud** : translated to Canterbury, 1633.
1633. **William Juxon** : attended Charles I. at his execution ; in 1660 Archbishop of Canterbury.
1660. **Gilbert Sheldon** : builder of the Sheldonian Theatre at Oxford. In 1663 Abp. of Canterbury.
1663. **Humphrey Henchman** : when Bishop of Salisbury. assisted escape of Charles II.
1664. William Sancroft, dean.
1665. The Great Plague.
1666. The Fire of London.
1675. **Henry Compton** : soldier, traveller, tutor to Mary and Anne. daughters of James II. ; insulted by Judge Jefferies ; the only prelate to sign petition to William of Orange ; preached at opening of the new Cathedral ; founder of the library.
1706. Sir John Evelyn, Wren's friend, died.
1710. Trial of Dr. Sacheverell.
1723. Death of Sir Christopher Wren, aged 91.
1791. Boswell's Life of Johnson published
1813. **William Howley** : Archbishop of Canterbury 1828 ; crowns the Queen 1837.
1815. Battle of Waterloo.
1828. **Charles James Blomfield** : resigned 1856.
1841. Ainsworth's "Old St. Paul's" published.
1849. Henry Hart Milman, dean.
1854. The Crimean War.
1856. **Archibald Campbell Tait.**
1863. **John Jackson.**
1869. Henry Longueville Mansel, dean.
1871. Richard William Church, dean.
1872. Thanksgiving Service for recovery of Prince of Wales.
1885. **Frederick Temple.**
1891. Robert Gregory, dean.
1896. **Mandell Creighton.**
1897. The Queen's Diamond Jubilee Service.
1901. Arthur Foley Winnington-Ingram.

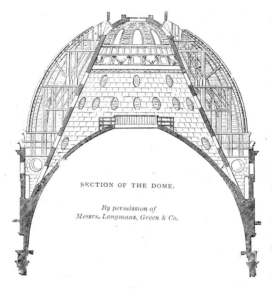

SECTION OF THE DOME.

*By permission of
Messrs. Longmans, Green & Co.*

DIMENSIONS OF CATHEDRAL.

External length, 515 feet. Of transepts 250 feet.
Diameter of dome at first stage about 140 feet. Height of
cross from ground 365 feet; western towers 221 feet.

THE LIBRARY.

WINCHESTER.

THE CATHEDRAL FROM ST. GILES' HILL.

WINCHESTER is famous among the many famous Cathedrals of our country. Its history begins in legendary times, and is full of interest. Lucius, king of the Britons, in 164 is said to have founded the first Christian Church, possibly on the very spot where a Pagan Temple had stood in the Roman Wintonia. This church was destroyed in 266, during the Diocletian persecution, but it was restored in 293 and then dedicated to St. Amphibalus. In 495 the Saxon invaders converted it into a temple of Dagon and it was not until 635 when Birinus, sent by Pope Honorius I, had converted the king, Kynegils, that Wessex once more was Christian. A new Church was now built, together with a monastery, the most famous prior of which in later times (852) was Swithun, Bishop, Lord Chancellor, and Weather Saint. Ethelwold in 963 rebuilt the Cathedral, and remains of his work are still pointed out in the crypt. Under "Building Dates" on another page the subsequent history of the building is traced.

To trace the connection of the Winchester Ecclesiastics and the Cathedral with the political life of our country is a study of the greatest interest. The Saxon Swithun was King Alfred's tutor; Walkelin, the first Norman Bishop, was a relative of the Conqueror; Henry de Blois, brother of Stephen, Peter des Roches, William Edington,

THE CATHEDRAL FROM THE AVENUE.

William of Wykeham, Cardinal Beaufort were all powerful statesmen; while in modern times the traditions of the see were amply sustained by Bishop Wilberforce.

It was from Winchester that Egbert's famous edict was issued in 828, ordering our island to be styled England, and its people Englishmen. Domesday Book was called the book of Winton. Many interesting events have of course taken place within the Cathedral walls. Henry I was here married to the English Matilda; King John was received back into the Church by Stephen Langton; a still more interesting scene was the marriage of Philip and Mary, the chair in which Mary sat is still to be seen in the Church. The Parliamentary army under Waller, including two troops of horse, marched into the Cathedral during service with colours and drums. They did irreparable damage, but this is readily forgiven when we remember the ever memorable incident of the old Wykehamist, Colonel Fiennes, standing with drawn sword to protect the Chantry of the Founder of his old school.

A statuette of Isaak Walton, the charm of whose book makes the reader forget for the time the cruelty of his sport, can be seen on the great screen. Jane Austen too, and Anthony Trollope are names recalled at Winchester; while not many miles away are Hursley, the home of Keble, and Eversley, the home of Winchester's immortal son, Charles Kingsley.

FEATURES TO BE NOTICED.

Longest Cathedral in England, and the longest Mediæval Cathedral in Europe. Plan same as St. Albans.

Compare work of transepts with the, later, piers of tower.

Vault of nave: about 350 feet, unsupported by flying buttresses. Compare Canterbury seven years later.

Transformation wrought by Wykeham. Compare nave and transepts. Norman arches to be found behind triforium.

Iron grill work door in N. aisle oldest in England.

Carving of choir-stalls best examples of the best period.

The Reredos: to be compared with those at Christchurch, St. Saviour's, Southwark, and St. Albans.

Norman Font. Mortuary chests in feretory. Glass of E. and W. Windows.

The Chantries finest in the Kingdom; an excellent series for study of change of style.

Old timber from roof now placed in N. transept.

In the library, a twelfth century Vulgate.

BUILDING DATES.

- 980. Ethelwold's Church; fragments in crypt.
- 1079. Bishop Walkelin begins to build the Cathedral on a new site; work completed 1093. Now existing, the transepts; cores of piers of nave; walls of nave, although much altered; the crypt. The nave ended with two huge towers, and extended to W. 40 feet beyond present building.
- 1107. Central tower fell.
- 1120. Rebuilding of central tower completed.
- 1150.c. The Font.
- 1175.c. Chapel of the Holy Sepulchre.
- 1202. Retro-choir begun by Bishop Lucy. The Guardian Angels chapel is Bishop Lucy's: as is also the S. chapel; the latter was transformed by Bishop Langton.
- 1296.c. The Stalls.
- 1320.c. Presbytery rebuilt; beautiful tabernacle work still remains.
- 1360. West front, and W. end of nave begun by Bishop Edington.
- 1394. Nave completely transformed by William of Wykeham. S. side completed before 1404. N. side completed 1486.
- 1475 (?). The Reredos—builder uncertain.
- 1487. Lady Chapel lengthened.
- 1500. Choir Pulpit—Prior Silkstede.
- 1520.c. Presbytery transformed by Bishop Fox. Relic chests of Feretory.
- 1563. Cloisters and Monastic buildings destroyed.
- 1634. Wooden groining to central tower.
- 1668. The Library.
  Porch at W. front restored.
- 1710. Throne of Corinthian design erected by Bishop Trelawney; subsequenly removed.
- 1782. Benjamin West's painting "The Raising of Lazarus" hung on reredos.
- 1875. Choir Screen altered by Sir Gilbert Scott.
- 1884. Nave Pulpit brought from New College.
- 1899. West's picture removed, and the reredos completed by the Crucifix, and with figures in the niches.

THE CHANTRIES.

1366. Bishop Edington.	1501. Bishop Langton.
1404. William of Wykeham.	1528. Bishop Fox.
1447. Cardinal Beaufort.	1555. Bishop Gardiner.
1486. Bishop Waynflete.	

MONUMENTS.

In addition to those mentioned under "Historical Notes," there are memorials, or tombs of James I and Charles I by Le Suer, the artist of the Charles I at Charing Cross; Mrs. Montague (1800), the founder of the "Blue Stocking" Club; Jane Austen, the novelist; Two brothers of Avington, note interesting inscription; Colonel Boles (1641) a brave soldier of Charles I; Isaak Walton (1683) the "compleat angler"; Sir Arnold de Gaveston, father of Piers Gaveston; Dr. Warton (Flaxman) Professor of Poetry at Oxford, head-master of Winchester; Sir John Clobery, one of those who helped in the restoration of Charles II; King William Rufus (?); Prior Silkstede; Earl of Portland, Lord High Treasurer to Charles I; Richard, Son of William I; Sir John Mason, the lay dean (1549-53); Prior William of Basing II (1284-95), mitred by the Pope to release him from episcopal discipline; and others of less interest.

The following-without monument also lie buried in the Cathedral: Kynegils, and Kenwarth, kings of Wessex; Egbert, Ethelwulf, Edward the Elder, and Edred; Cnut, and Harthacnut; William Rufus; St. Birinus, St. Swithun, Archbishop Stigand, and Bishops Ethelwulf, Walkelin, and Gifford; Queen Emma, and Earl Godwin.

DIMENSIONS OF CATHEDRAL.

Total internal length, 556 feet. Breadth of nave and aisles, 88 feet. Height of walls, 75 feet; tower, 140 feet.

THE FONT.

THE NAVE.

NORTH TRANSEPT.

WYKEHAM'S CHANTRY

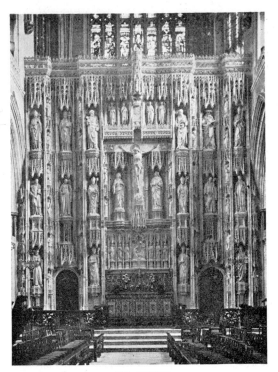

THE REREDOS.

THE CHOIR STALLS.

S. AISLE OF RETRO-CHOIR.

THE EAST END.

HISTORICAL NOTES.

Bishops' names are in heavy letter.   Monuments are noted*.

A.D.

43-410. ROMAN OCCUPATION OF BRITAIN.

164. King Lucius said to have rebuilt Church.

449. ENGLISH LAND IN BRITAIN.

520. Kingdom of Wessex established.

597. Augustine lands in Kent.

634. Mission of Birinus.

679. Bishop's seat removed to Winchester from Dorchester in Oxfordshire.

787. DANES FIRST LAND IN ENGLAND.

827. Egbert Overlord of all England.

852. **Swithun**: Prior and subsequently Bishop; remembered as a weather saint—on July 15th.

963. **Ethelwold**: bishop for 21 years; moved the body of St. Swithun on July 15th, 980.

985. **Alphege**: subsequently Archbishop of Canterbury.

1032. **Alwin**: the legendary lover of Queen Emma.

1047. **Stigand**: in 1052 Archbishop of Canterbury.

1066. NORMAN CONQUEST OF ENGLAND.

1070. **Walkelin**: first Norman Bishop; rebuilt Cathedral.

1100.	**William Gifford**:	founder of St. Saviour's, Southwark, and Waverley Abbey—Sir W. Scott's Waverley.
(?) *1119.	**Henry de Blois**:	grandson of the Conqueror, and brother of King Stephen; consecrated Becket as Archbishop; founded hospital of St. Cross.
1174.	**Richard Toclive**:	an opponent of Becket, but after the murder dedicated churches to him.
(?) *1189.	**Godfrey de Lucy**:	built the retro-choir; improved the navigation of river Itchin.
(?) *1204.	**Peter des Roches**:	a partisan of King John; a Crusader; founded the Domus Dei at Portsmouth, and the monastery at Selborne.
1215.	Magna Charta--June 15th.	
1220.	The Friars arrive in England.	
*1250.	**Ethelmar or Aylmer de Valance**:	an unpopular, rapacious and tyranical bishop.
*1268.	**Nicholas of Ely**:	once Lord Chancellor and High Treasurer.
1305.	**Henry Woodlock**:	crowned Edward II.
1323.	**John Stratford**:	later Abp. of Canterbury.
1324.	William of Wykeham born.	
1333.	**Adam Orlton**:	said (probably unjustly) to have instigated the murder of Edward II.
*1346.	**William Edington**:	First Chancellor of the Order of the Garter; Treasurer of England 1350; Chancellor 1357.
1366.	Wycliffe defends refusal of subsidy to Rome.	
*1367.	**William of Wykeham**:	rebuilt the nave of Cathedral; founded Winchester school, and New College, Oxford; his name is known in connection with building at Windsor and other great castles; his motto—"Manners Makyth Man," throughout the world.
*1405.	**Henry of Beaufort**:	son of John of Gaunt, thrice Chancellor of England; rebuilt and re-endowed St. Cross, an "Almhouse of Noble Poverty"; devoted an immense amount of money to the inmates of London prisons; tried Jeanne d' Arc; the Bishop of Shakespeare's Henry VI.
*1447.	**William of Waynflete**:	founder of Magdalen College, Oxford.
1474.	CAXTON SETTLES IN ENGLAND.	
*1487.	**Peter Courtenay.**	
*1493.	**Thomas Langton**:	a great educationist.

*1500. **Richard Fox**: founder of Corpus Christi College, Oxford.

1529. **Thomas Wolsey**: one year "in commendam."

*1531. **Stephen Gardiner**: the cruel persecutor of Queen Mary's reign; deprived 1550, restored 1553.

1550. **John Poynet**: a great helper of Cranmer with the first Prayer Book.

1554. Marriage of Queen Mary and Philip of Spain.

1556. **John White**: deposed by Queen Elizabeth.

1588. DEFEAT OF THE SPANISH ARMADA.

1596. **William Day**: provost of Eton for 34 years.

1597. **Thomas Bilson**: a Bible reviser.

1619. **Lancelot Andrewes**: a learned preacher; Bible reviser; buried at St. Saviour's, Southwark.

1627. **Richard Neile**: later, Archbishop of York.

1632. **Walter Curle**: a follower of Laud.

1645. Winchester finally taken by Cromwell.

1650. See vacant for ten years.

1660. **Brian Duppa**: chaplain to Charles I., accompanied him to Carisbrooke Castle.

*1662. **George Morley**: founded the Cathedral library; a friend of Isaak Walton.

*1684. **Peter Mews**: a captain in the Civil War; fought at Sedgmoor against Monmouth.

1707. **Sir Jonathan Trelawney**: tried as one of the "Seven Bishops."

1721. **Charles Trimnell**: an opponent of Sacheverell.

*1723. **Richard Willis**: a strong advocate for repeal of the Test and Corporation Acts.

*1734. **Benjamin Hoadly**: favourite of George I.

1761. **John Thomas**: tutor to George III.

1781. **Brownlow North**: half-brother of Lord North.

*1820. **Sir George Pretyman Tomline**: distinguished scholar, and tutor to Pitt.

*1827. **Charles Sumner**: first bishop since Reformation to be enthroned at Winchester.

*1869. **Samuel Wilberforce**: son of William Wilberforce; famous as bishop of Oxford; a warm supporter of Mr. Gladstone.

1873. **Edward Harold Brown.**

*1890. **Anthony Wilson Thorold.**

1895. **Randall Thomas Davidson.**

THE RETRO-CHOIR.

TRANSEPT AND EAST END.

GLOUCESTER.

THE CATHEDRAL FROM THE RIVER SEVERN.

O F the first introduction of Christianity to Gloucester, the Roman Glevum, nothing authentic is known. A very doubtful legend attributes its establishment to King Lucius, but history does not begin until 681. An abbey was then founded by Osric, viceroy of King Ethelred of Mercia, for monks and nuns, ruled by an abbess, Kyneburga, the sister of Osric, being the first. Eva was her successor, and when she died in 769 the establishment was broken up. About 823 Beornwulf, King of Mercia, rebuilt the monastery, and introduced secular priests; these in 1022 were changed by Cnut to Benedictines. The monastery was burnt down in 1058, but was rebuilt and reformed by Aldred, Bishop of Worcester. When the Norman Serlo became Abbot in 1072 there were however only two monks, and eight novices; but under his influence the numbers rapidly increased, and rebuilding became necessary. The work was begun in 1089, some of the materials, as at St. Albans, being taken from the Roman wall. It inaugurated a period of four hundred years of building activity, resulting in the completion of one of the most beautiful, and, architecturally, one of the most interesting of our cathedrals. The chief interest of Gloucester Cathedral is architectural, but there is a strong human side. John Hooper, Bishop of Gloucester, was one of the first four victims of the Marian persecutions: Robert Raikes, the father of the Sunday

THE CATHEDRAL FROM THE SOUTH-WEST.

School was a Gloucester man. The Conqueror spent his
Christmas at Gloucester when possible; it was from this
city that he issued his command for the compilation of
Domesday Book. Here William Rufus forced the Archbishopric upon Anselm. Parliaments were held in the
great hall of the abbey by Henry I., Edward I., Richard
II., Henry IV. and V., and it is said that it was at
Gloucester that Richard III. decreed the murder of his
nephews. Abbot Thokey, braving the anger of the Queen,
received the body of the murdered King Edward II., whose
monument became a place of pilgrimage, the offerings
at which brought an enormous revenue to the monastery.
At the Dissolution of the Monastries the abbey church
became a cathedral, and John Wakeman, Abbot of
Tewksbury, the first bishop. Not much damage was
done during the Civil War, but later on an attempt
was made to pull down parts of the building. Happily
this was arrested, and further desecration was avoided by
the church being given to the City.

FEATURES TO BE NOTICED.

The birth-place of the Perpendicular style. Clothing
of Norman work with Perpendicular, especially in choir,
of great interest and beauty.

Unusual height of nave piers.

Choir partly above tower.

Lady Chapel one of the largest in the kingdom.

Construction of building connecting choir and Lady
Chapel.

The Whispering Gallery.

Cloisters the finest in the kingdom.

East window (five feet wider than choir walls) is the
largest in the world—72 × 38 or 2736 square feet. York
East window is 78 × 33 or 2574 but has more glass than
Gloucester.

Old Tiles, especially in presbytery and Lady Chapel.

The Central Tower; to be compared with Canterbury
which is 10 feet higher, and about 50 years later.

Monastic buildings and cloisters on north side of
church, instead of on the, usual, south side.

BUILDING DATES.

1089. Present Cathedral begun by Abbot Serlo: the work of E. end remains.
1100. Dedication of the E. end of the building.
1101. Damage by fire.
1122. Another fire, destroying roof of nave.
    Abbey buildings surrounded by stone wall.
    Crypt strengthened by masonry.
    Prior's lodge; the crypt and slype.
1170c. Fall of western tower.
    New stalls in choir—only fragments remain.
    All work to this date except the W. end practically remains, but with great alteration and addition.
1222. Great eastern tower—no trace remaining.
1225. Lady Chapel; rebuilt 1457-99.
1242. Nave triforium altered; nave vaulted.
1300. Another fire.
1318c. South aisle of nave reconstructed by Abbot Thokey.
1327. Edward II. interred in the church.
1330c. South transept reconstructed.
1337-51. Choir cased and vaulted by Adam de Staunton.
    Stalls on Prior's (N.) side.
1350.c. The east window.
1351-77. Thomas Horton completed Staunton's work, including the presbytery, the high altar, and stalls on Abbot's (S.) side. He also completed transformation of N. transept, built some monastic buildings, and part of cloisters.
1381-1407. Cloisters completed by Abbot Froucester.
1421-37. West front, and W. end of nave rebuilt by Abbot Mouvent.
    South Porch.
    Windows of nave clerestory.
1440c. Abbot Boteler's chapel.
1450-57. Central tower begun by Abbot Seabroke; completed by a monk, Robert Tully.
1457-72. Eastern bay of chapter-house.
    Lady Chapel begun, Abbot Hanley; completed by Abbot Farley before 1498.
    John the Baptist's chapel.
1576. Considerable repairs.
1616. Restorations begun by Laud.
1710. Wooden reredos; replaced 1807, and again 1873.
1740c. Nave paved, and other works carried out by Bishop Benson.
1820. Choir screen; replacing Bishop Benson's.
1847. Restoration begun under Mr. F. S. Waller.

1853. Sir Gilbert Scott at work.
1862. East window restored.
1867. St. Andrew's chapel painted by Mr. Gambier Parry.
1896. Lady Chapel restored.

MONUMENTS.

In addition to those mentioned under "Historical Notes," there are, among others, monuments or tombs of King Osric; (?) Robert, Duke of Normandy; Edward II; John de Staunton, brother of the Abbot; John Jones, M.P. for Gloucester at time of Gunpowder Plot, and registrar to eight bishops; Mrs. Morley (1784) (*Flaxman*) who died at sea with her young child; Rev. **Thomas Stock**, a worker with Robert Raikes; Sir George O. Paul (1820), an active worker for prison reform; Dr. Jenner (1823), the discoverer of vaccination; Rev. H. Haines (1872), for 23 years a master in the Cathedral school; Dr. S. S. Wesley (1876) the distinguished organist of the Cathedral.

DIMENSIONS OF CATHEDRAL.

External length 425 feet; Tower 225. Internal length of nave 174; choir 140; Lady Chapel 90. Width of nave 34; aisles 15; across transepts 128.

THE NAVE.

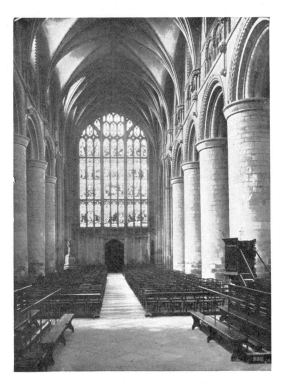

THE NAVE, LOOKING W.

THE CHOIR.

THE SOUTH TRIFORIUM.

THE SOUTH AMBULATORY.

THE LADY CHAPEL

THE CRYPT.

Historical Notes.

Abbots' and Bishops' names are in heavy letter. Monuments are noted*.

A.D.

43-410. ROMAN OCCUPATION OF BRITAIN.
    Glevum (Gloucester) walled by the Romans.

201. King Lucius died at Gloucester.

449. ENGLISH LAND IN BRITAIN.

577. Battle of Deorham.

597. Augustine lands in Kent.

681. First Abbey founded by Osric.

787. DANES FIRST LAND IN ENGLAND.

821. Beornwulf, King of Mercia, said to have established secular priests, and to have rebuilt the Monastery.

1022. King Cnut introduced Benedictine monks.

1066. NORMAN CONQUEST OF ENGLAND.

1072. **Serlo**: first Norman Abbot; chaplain of the Conqueror.

1086. Domesday Book completed.

1093. Anselm consecrated Archbishop of Canterbury at Gloucester.

1131. **Walter de Lacy**: Robert, Duke of Normandy dying (1134) during his rule, was buried in the choir.

1139. **Gilbert Foliot**: Bishop of Hereford 1148; of London 1163; supported the King against Becket.

1216. Henry III. crowned in the church.

1283. Foundation of Gloucester Hall, Oxford, on the site of Worcester College.

1284. Edward, first Prince of Wales, born.

1298. Chronicle of Robert of Gloucester.

1306. **John Thokey**: builder of S. aisle of nave received the body of Edward II. for interment.

1327. Murder of Edward II. at Berkeley Castle.

1329. **John Wygemore**: began the great architectural changes of the building.

1381. **Walter Froucester**: chronicler of the Cathedral; builder of the greater part of the cloisters; mitred by Pope Urban VI.

1420. **John Morwent**: rebuilt W. end of the church.

*1450. **Thomas Seabroke**: builder of the tower.

1472. **William Farley**: builder of Lady Chapel.

1474. CAXTON SETTLES IN ENGLAND.

*1515. **William Malverne or Parker;** the last abbot.

1534. PAPAL SUPREMACY ABOLISHED IN ENGLAND.

1536. English Bible issued.

THE MORLEY MONUMENT.

1539. SUPPRESSION OF THE GREATER ABBEYS,
including Gloucester.

1541. Episcopal See of Gloucester founded by separation
from Worcester.

John Wakeman: first bishop; abbot of
Tewksbury; revised the Revelation in Cranmer's
Bible.

1551. **John Hooper**: surrendered office 1552 but reappointed to the united sees of Gloucester and Worcester; deprived and imprisoned by Mary 1553; burnt as heretic February 9th, 1555.

1554. Gloucester again separated from Worcester.

1605. **Thomas Ravis**: a translator of part of New Testament of James I. Bible.

1605. Gunpowder Plot.

1611. AUTHORIZED BIBLE PUBLISHED.

1612. **Miles Smith**: translated the Prophets in James I. Bible, and wrote the Preface.

1625. **Godfrey Goodman**: suspected of Romanism, and suspended by Laud 1640; restored. and again deprived by Parliament; died 1656; buried in St. Margaret's, Westminster.

1646c. Sect of Quakers founded by G. Fox.

1661. **William Nicolson**: first bishop of Restoration.

1681. **Robert Frampton**: a Nonjuror, and deprived.

1691. **Edward Fowler**: a Latitudinarian.

1715. **Richard Willis**: to Salisbury 1721; Winchester 1725; strong advocate for repeal of the Test and Corporation Acts.

1721. **John Wilcocks**: in 1731 to Rochester, and to deanery of Westminster.

1724. Music Festival of Three Choirs founded.

1735. **Martin Benson**: an extensive "repairer." of the Cathedral.

Robert Raikes born.

1760. **William Warburton**: friend of Pope; author of "The Divine Legation of Moses," etc. Dr. Johnson wrote in his praise.

1779. **James Yorke**: son of Ld. Chancellor Hardwicke.

1780. SUNDAY SCHOOLS ESTABLISHED by Robert Raikes.

1796. Dr. Jenner's first experiment in vaccination.

1815. **Henry Ryder**; to Lichfield 1824, where is his well-known monument by Chantrey.

1827. Gloucester and Berkeley canal completed.

1830. **James Henry Monk**: under his rule (1836.) the sees of Bristol and Gloucester were united.

1856. **Charles Baring**: to Durham 1861. "*John Halifax*" published.

1861. **William Thomson**: Archbishop of York 1862.

1863. **Charles J. Ellicott,** chairman of the New Testament Revision Committee.

1881. REVISED NEW TESTAMENT PUBLISHED.

1898. Separation of Sees of Gloucester and Bristol.

THE CLOISTER.

BISHOP HOOPER'S MONUMENT.

LICHFIELD.

THE CATHEDRAL FROM SOUTH EAST.

THE kingdom of Mercia was one of the last parts of England to embrace Christianity. Peada, son of Penda, king of Mercia, as a condition of marriage to the daughter of the Christian king, Oswi, of Northumbria, was converted. Returning home with his bride he took with him four priests who, with consent of Penda, laboured at converting the people. Diuma, an Irish Scot, was one of the four, and was made the first Bishop of Mercia by Oswi, who in 655 overthrew Penda in battle. But the place of the see was not fixed until 669 when the famous Ceadda, better known as St. Chad, became bishop. He built the first church on or near the site of the present Cathedral. No trace of this remains, nor of the second church, to which the body of the saint was later on translated. Under Bishop Saxulf, 675-91, Mercia was divided into five sees—Lichfield, Hereford, Worcester, Leicester, and Lindsey. The last two were subsequently merged in Lincoln. In 775 Offa became king of Mercia and ten years later obtained from the Pope the dignity of an archbishopric for his kingdom, the Archbishop of Lichfield having under his rule six suffragans, leaving four only to Canterbury. In 803 however the act was annulled.

THE WEST FRONT.

The first Norman bishop, Peter, removed the seat of the see to Chester; his successor removed it again to Coventry, and it was not until 1128 that a return was made to Lichfield.

In the Civil War the close, which had been fortified by Bishop Walter Langton, was held for the king against the Parliamentarians under Lord Brooke. On March 2nd, 1643, St. Chad's Day, "a shot from the battlement of the great spire by one deaf and dumb Dyott" killed Lord Brooke, and a tablet in Dam Street marks the spot where he fell. Sir John Gell succeeded to the command, and his guns brought down the central spire. When the garrison surrendered on March 5th the church was despoiled in the manner characteristic of the times. There was another siege by Prince Rupert a month later, and a third in 1646 by Parliamentary forces. After the restoration, Bishop Hacket began to repair the damage; and the central spire was rebuilt from designs of Sir Christopher Wren. The subsequent history is uneventful, but an increasing appreciation of the Cathedral has preserved it one of the most beautiful in the country.

FEATURES TO BE NOTICED.

The colour of the stone; red sandstone.

The three spires, "Ladies of the Vale."

West Front, one of the three best in England, and especially the door; the large window is modern (1869) replacing Bishop Hacket's.

One of the smallest Cathedrals in England.

Orientation of nave and choir different.

Unusual size of triforium compared with pier arches and clerestory.

Clever juncture of Early English and Decorated work of choir.

Richness of the carving throughout the building.

Glass of Lady Chapel.

Woodwork of choir executed by Mr. Evans, the original of Seth in "Adam Bede."

In the library are the "Gospels of St. Chad."

BUILDING DATES.

Of the Saxon churches there are no remains, and only fragments of the first Norman church.

1200.c. Choir of present Cathedral begun. Now existing, lower portions of three western bays.

1220c. South transept begun.

1240.c. North transept and Chapter House begun.

1250.c. Nave: Central tower probably rebuilt.

1275.c. West Front begun; the two towers were not completed until about 1330, and the spires later still.

1300.c. Lady Chapel begun by Walter Langton.
Shrine of St. Chad—destroyed in Civil War.
The close fortified with a stone wall—no remains.
Bishop's palace, destroyed in Civil War.

1330.c. Presbytery, and clerestory of choir rebuilt.

1340.c. Lady Chapel completed by Roger Norburgh.

1457.c. The Library built by Dean Heywood; removed 1750

1642. General wreck of the Cathedral during siege, including destruction of central spire.

1661. Restoration begun by Bishop Hacket.

1687. The Bishop's Palace: the wings and chapel later.

1760. Wyatt's restorations: Screen dividing Lady Chapel from Choir removed.

1802. Glass of Lady Chapel brought from Herckenrode.

1822. West Front filled with Roman cement figures by Dean Woodhouse: removed 1877.

1856. Sir Gilbert Scott's restorations begun.

1884. Restoration of West Front completed.

MONUMENTS.

In addition to those mentioned under "Historical Notes" there are monuments or tombs of Lady Mary Wortly Montague (1762) the introducer to this country of inoculation; Gilbert Walmesly the friend of Dr. Johnson; Dean Addison (1703) father of a more famous son; Dean Heywood (1492) a great benefactor of the Cathedral; Dean Woodhouse (1833); Dr. Johnson (1784); David Garrick (1779); Andrew Newton (1806), benefactor of town and Cathedral; Archdeacon Hodson (1855), father of Major Hodson, and of the present esteemed Vicar of Enfield; Major Hodson (1858) of "Hodson's Horse" fame; Erasmas Darwin (1802) grandfather of Charles Darwin; Archdeacon Moore (1876); Dean Howard (1868); Dean Bickersteth (1892); "The Sleeping Children," the famous work of Chantry.

WEST DOOR.

DIMENSIONS OF CATHEDRAL.

Central spire 252 feet.
Western spires 195 feet.
Length 370 feet.

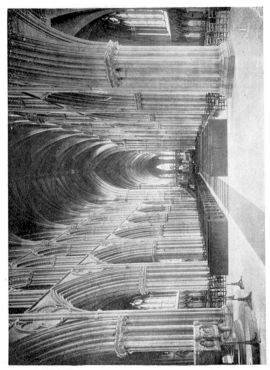

THE NAVE

CHOIR, LOOKING WEST.

THE REREDOS.

ST. CHAD'S CHAPEL.

NORTH AISLE OF NAVE.

EAST END OF CHAPTER HOUSE.

THE "SLEEPING CHILDREN."

Historical Notes.

Bishops' names are in heavy letter. Monuments are noted *

A.D.

43-410. ROMAN OCCUPATION OF BRITAIN.
First introduction of Christianity.

400. Ninian settles in the Lowlands of Scotland.

449. ENGLISH LAND IN BRITAIN.

565. Columba settles in Iona.

597. Augustine lands in Kent.

633. King Penda wins battle of Hatfield, and enlarges kingdom of Mercia.

653. Conversion of the Mercians.

656. **Diuma**: first bishop of Mercia.

669. **Ceadda**: fixed place of see at Lichfield, and subsequently, as **St. Chad**, became the patron saint.

673. Synod of Hertford.

675. Mercia divided into five sees.

779. Higbert: made Archbishop by the Pope at Offa's instigation.

790. Offa establishes monastery of St. Albans.

803. Lichfield again becomes a suffragan see.

1066. NORMAN CONQUEST OF ENGLAND.

1072. **Peter**: first Norman bishop; removed the place of see to Chester.

1086. **Robert de Limesey**: removed the place of see to Coventry where Earl Leofric and Lady Godiva had founded their great monastery.

1129. **Roger de Clinton**: from his time bishops are designated of Lichfield and Coventry.

1188. **Hugh Monant**: Clerk of Thomas Becket; partisan of John, deprived and restored by Richard I.; fierce opponent of monks.

1215. **William of Cornhill**: consecrated by Archbishop S. Langton on same day as Bishop Poer, afterwards of Salisbury.

1215. Magna Charta, June 15th.

1224. **Alexander Stavenby**: during his rule decree was made that monks of Coventry, and canons of Lichfield should alternately elect bishop.

*1240. **Hugh Patteshull**: Treasurer of England.

1258. **Roger de Meyland**: son of Earl William Longespée of Salisbury; utterly neglected diocese, spending most of his time abroad.

*1296. **Walter Langton**: Keeper of Great Seal; Treasurer of England; executor of the will of Edward I.; imprisoned by Edward II., but released by demand of the clergy; great benefactor of the Cathedral, founding the Lady Chapel, and new shine of St. Chad, and a new palace.

1322. **Roger Northburgh**: captured by the Scots at Bannockburn in 1314; Treasurer of England.

1360. **Robert Stretton**: chaplain to the Black Prince; an illiterate.

1386. **Richard Scrope**: translated to York 1398 and there beheaded; the Archbishop of Shakespeare's Henry IV.

1452. **Nicholas Close**: one of the six original *scolares*, and master of the works of King's College, Cambridge; chancellor of Cambridge.

1474. CAXTON SETTLES IN ENGLAND.

1492. **William Smyth**: founder of Brasenose College.

1534. **Rowland Lee**: secured the full Parliamentary rights of Wales, Chester, and Monmouth.

1567. Rugby School founded by Lawrence Sheriff.

1609. **George Abbott**: to London 1610; Canterbury 1611; translated the four Gospels, and the Acts in "King James's Bible;" founded a hospital at Guildford.

1610.	**Richard Neile**: a friend of Lord Burghley; he burnt a "heretic" in 1611; Dean of Westminster (1562); Bishop of Rochester (1608); Lincoln (1613); Durham (1617); Winchester (1627); Archbishop of York (1631).
1619.	**Thomas Morton**: zealous in his conversion of Papists and Nonconformists; translated to Durham where he had a noble and distinguished career, he died in 1659 aged 95.
1642.	Sieges of Cathedral.
1644.	**Accepted Frewen**: consecrated in Chapel of Magdalen College, Oxford; Archbishop of York 1660.
1645.	Execution of Archbishop Laud.
	Charles I. visits Lichfield after Naseby.
1649.	Execution of Charles I.
*1661.	**John Hacket**: the restorer of the Cathedral after the damage done during the War.
1692.	**William Lloyd**: tried as one of the "Seven Bishops."
1699.	**John Hough**: the President of Magdalen College deposed by James II.
1709.	Samuel Johnson born at Lichfield September 18th.
1712.	Dr. Sacheverell at Lichfield.
1745.	Charles Edward marches to Derby.
1750.	**Frederick Cornwallis**; translated to Canterbury, 768.
1760.	John Wesley visits Burslem.
1766.	Grand Trunk canal begun by Brindley.
1769.	Josiah Wedgwood opens works at Etruria.
1775.	**Richard Hurd**: born at Penkridge; biographer of Warburton.
1776.	Dr. Johnson and Boswell visit Lichfield.
1781.	**James, Earl of Cornwallis.**
1789.	The French Revolution.
*1824.	**Henry Ryder**: brother of the Earl of Harrowby
1836.	**Samuel Butler**: began as Bishop of Lichfield and Coventry, ended as Bishop of Lichfield.
1840.	**James Bowstead.**
*1843.	**John Lonsdale.**
1847.	Trent Valley Railway opened.
1857.	Indian Mutiny.
1859.	"Adam Bede" published.
1860.	Sir Gilbert Scott's restorations begun.
*1868.	**George Augustus Selwyn.**
1871.	Martyrdom of Bishop Patteson in Melanesia
1878.	**William Dalrymple Maclagan**: Archbishop of York 1891.
1891.	**Hon. Augustus Legge.**

LADY CHAPEL.

THE EAST END.

SALISBURY.

THE CATHEDRAL FROM THE SOUTH-WEST.

VERY few English cathedrals have received the unstinted praise that has been bestowed upon Salisbury. It is well deserved. The beautiful and peaceful situation, the wonderful harmony of the building, and the marvellous spire are all most impressive, and charm the visitor. There is of course the greatest possible interest to be found in the study of the alterations and additions made to the Mediæval cathedrals, but it is good to have at least one building that speaks, and that so beautifully, one thought.

The history of the See commences with the foundation of the bishopric of Sherborne in 705. Two hundred years later, in 909, a new diocese was created for Wiltshire alone, with its seat at Ramsbury or Wilton. So things continued until Norman times, when Bishop Herman united the sees of Sherborne and Wilton, placing his seat at Old Sarum. Of this diocese Osmund, the compiler of the "Use of Sarum" is the best remembered bishop. He completed the Cathedral which, however, was not destined to have so long a history as other Norman buildings. Bishop Poore decided on removing to the present site, and in 1220 the building as we now know it was begun, three altars being completed in 1225. Three years later Bishop Poore was translated to Durham. His successor, however, energetically carried on the work, and in 1258 the whole building was

THE WEST FRONT.

finished, at a cost, at present value, of about half a million. The spire was added about one hundred years later. Since then there have been renovations and restorations, and certain strengthening work, but the beautiful church has survived them all, and is substantially as its builders left it, the most perfect example of the period.

The Cathedral is not very rich in architectural monuments, but there are a good many of interest, particularly those of two famous earls. William Longespée (1226), Earl of Salisbury, the son of Henry II. and Fair Rosamond, took an active part in State affairs during the reign of John, and was a witness to Magna Carta, a copy of which is in the library. A Crusader himself, he transmitted his warlike tastes to his son, who joined two Crusades, and falling near Cairo in 1250, was buried at Acre. The monument in the Cathedral is said to have been erected by his mother, the Countess Ella.

It is of interest to know that Bishop Poore is said to have planned the parochial divisions of the City of Salisbury, and that they remained practically unaltered until the end of the nineteenth century. Now a change has been made, a new parish—St. Mark's, has been formed, and one of the most beautiful of modern churches has been erected.

FEATURES TO BE NOTICED.

The beauty of the site, and the proportions of the building. No other church has stood on the site.

Plan: a double cross.

Spire: highest in England, and the most beautiful in the world; thickness of walls 2 feet to a height of 20 feet, and then only 9 inches; 23 inches out of perpendicular.

Regularity of size of stones, and even bands in building.

Number of windows is said to equal the days of the year; the pillars the hours; and the doorways the months.

Connected base of columns of main arcade.

Strengthening arches across transepts, the east different to west. To be compared with work at Wells and Canterbury.

Monuments to the earliest bishops some of the earliest of their class in England.

Consecration crosses on exterior walls.

Ball Flower not found on the earliest (E. end) building, but appears on W. front and tower.

Exterior view from N.E.

BUILDING DATES.

1220. Foundations laid by Bishop Poore.
1225. Three altars finished and consecrated.
1258. The whole building with exception of central tower
      and west front completed.
1263.c. Cloisters and Chapter House begun; completed
       about ten years later.
1326.c. Walls of Close begun.
1330.c. Two stages added to central tower.
1350.c. The Spire. Date is very uncertain,
1460.c. Strengthening arches across transepts.
1668. Restorations of Bishop Ward.
1789. Beauchamp and Hungerford Chapels and Campanile
      taken down; considerable alterations made under
      Wyatt.
1863. Sir Gilbert Scott's restorations begun.
1880. North Porch restored by Mr. G. E. Street.
1898. Tower restored under Dean Boyle by Sir Arthur
      Blomfield—cost £14,000.

DIMENSIONS OF CATHEDRAL.

Total exterior length 473 feet; nave 229½ feet. Interior
    height of nave 84 feet. Width of nave 82 feet.
    Central Spire 404 feet.

MONUMENTS.

In addition to those mentioned under "Historical
Notes," there are monuments, or tombs of Robert, Lord
Hungerford (1459) served in France under the Regent Duke
of Bedford; Lord Stourton (1556) hanged in the market place
for murder; William Longespée, Earl of Salisbury, son
of Henry II and Fair Rosamond; Sir John Cheyney (1509)
standard bearer f Henry at Bosworth; William Longespée,
fourth Earl of Salisbury, twice a Crusader, fell near Cairo
1250; the Boy Bishop (?); Sir John de Montacute (1389)
present at Crecy; Edward, Earl of Hertford, son of
Protector Somerset, and his wife, sister of Lady Jane Grey;
Isaak Walton, son of the "compleat angler"; Richard
Jefferies (1887) the author; Henry Fawcett, M.P. (1884);
John Britton (1857) author of series on Cathedrals of
England; Richard Hooker (1600) author of Ecclesiastical
Polity; and many others of great interest. In pavement
in front of the altar-rail, "Sidney's sister, Pembroke's
mother."

THE CATHEDRAL FROM THE NORTH-EAST.

THE CHOIR SCREEN.

THE CHOIR.

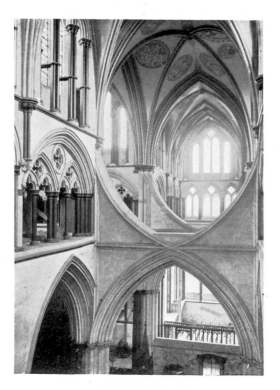

EAST TRANSEPTS.

WEST TRANSEPTS.

BISHOP BRIDPORT'S TOMB.

THE LADY CHAPEL.

NAVE TRIFORIUM.

Historical Notes.

Bishops' names are in heavy letter. Monuments are noted*.

A.D.

43-410. ROMAN OCCUPATION OF BRITAIN.
      Sorbiodunum (Old Sarum) established.
      First introduction of Christianity.
449. ENGLISH LAND IN BRITAIN.
520. Kingdom of Wessex established.
597. Augustine lands in Kent.
634. Mission of Birinus.
705. See of Sherborne founded.
      Aldhelm: first bishop; afterwards St. Aldhelm.
787. DANES FIRST LAND IN ENGLAND.
817. **Ealhstan**: a leader against the invaders.
868. **Heahmund**: killed in battle of Merton.
879. Peace of Wedmore.
909. **Werstan**: removed place of see to Wilton.
*1058. **Herman**: united sees of Wilton and Sherborne at
      Old Sarum in 1075 and began Cathedral there.
1066. NORMAN CONQUEST OF ENGLAND.
1078. **Osmund**: relative of the Conqueror; compiler of
      of the "Use of Sarum"; afterwards St. Osmund.
*1102. **Roger**: powerful statesman of Henry I; false to
      Matilda, mistrusted and imprisoned by Stephen.

*1142. **Jocelyn**: an opponent of Becket; probably framed the Constitutions of Clarendon.

1188. **Hubert Fitz Walter**: a Crusader; afterwards Archbishop of Canterbury.

1215. MAGNA CARTA.

*1217. **Richard Poore**: began the present Cathedral in 1220; translated to Durham 1228.

*1228. **Robert Bingham**: contd. work of Bishop Poore.

*1256. **Giles of Bridport**: during his rule the new cathedral was consecrated.

*1262. **Walter de la Wyle**: founded church of St. Edmund, Salisbury.

*1329. **Robert Wyvil**: appointed at instance of Queen Philippa; ugly and unlettered; he had a mansion in Fleet Street, London, now Salisbury Court.

1388. **John Waltham**: Master of the Rolls; Keeper of Privy Seal; Lord High Treasurer; resisted unsuccessfully the visitation of Archbishop Courtenay; buried in Westminster Abbey.

*1395. **Richard Mitford**: confessor of Richard II.

1408. **Robert Hallam**: Chancellor of Oxford; Cardinal 1411; English representative at Council of Constance; opposed the burning of heretics.

1438. **William Ayscough**: murdered during the Peasant Rising.

*1450. **Richard Beauchamp**: employed in various diplomatic missions; in 1477 Dean of Windsor; under him St. George's Chapel was built; disputes with Bp. Edington of Winchester the honour of being first Chancellor of the Order of the Garter; built the great hall and chapel of the bishop's palace.

1474. CAXTON SETTLES IN ENGLAND.

*1482. **Lionel Woodville**: nephew of Elizabeth, queen of Edward IV; said to have died of grief at downfall of the fortunes of his house.

*1502. **Edmund Audley**: son of Lord Audley; presented pulpit to St. Mary's Oxford.

1524. **Lorenzo Campeggio**: Cardinal of St. Anastasius; an adjudicator upon Henry VIII's divorce; deprived 1534 on the fall of Wolsey.

1535. **Nicholas Shaxton**: condemned as a heretic, recanted; preacher of fiery sermons at martyrdom of Anne Askew and others; buried in Gonville Hall.

*1539. **John Capon or Salcot**: a ready changer in changing times; a reviser of the liturgy under Edward VI; a judge of Bishop Hooper under Mary; a plunderer of his See.

*1560. **John Jewel**: first Protestant bishop; a diligent Reformer; Public Orator at Oxford; published in 1562 his "Apology of the Church of England"; preached at Paul's Cross against Cartwright and the Puritans; sent Richard Hooker to Oxford.

*1571. **Edmund Gheast**: furnished library with books.

1577. **John Piers**: preached before Queen Elizabeth thanksgiving sermon for defeat of the Armada.

1588. DEFEAT OF THE SPANISH ARMADA.

1591. **John Coldwell**: the first married bishop of Salisbury; Sir Walter Raleigh obtained from him Sherborne Castle.

1641. **Brian Duppa**: tutor to sons of Charles I.; accompanied the King to Carisbrooke; deprived by Parliament; to Winchester 1660.

1660. **Humphrey Henchman**: assisted Charles to escape after Worcester.

1663. **John Earle**: the companion of Charles in his wanderings; in 1660 bishop of Worcester.

*1667. **Seth Ward**: the repairer of the Cathedral after Civil War, employed Sir Christopher Wren to make survey; noted for his learning and charity.

1688. WILLIAM OF ORANGE LANDS AT TORBAY.

1689. **Gilbert Burnet**: author of "History of his Own Times"; the friend of William III.

1734. **Thomas Sherlock**: a powerful preacher; translated to London 1749.

1776. John Constable, painter, born.

1791. **John Douglas**: a Scotchman; as chaplain, present at battle of Fontenoy; prepared for publication Captain Cook's Journals.

*1807. **John Fisher**: tutor to Princess Charlotte.

1825. **Thomas Burgess**: founded Lampeter Coll.

*1837. **Edward Denison**: brother of Mr. Speaker Denison.

*1854. **Walter Kerr Hamilton**: founded Theological Coll.

*1869. **George Moberly**: Head Master Winchester 1835-1866.

1870. Elementary Education Act.

1881. Revised Version of New Testament published.

1885. **John Wordsworth.**

1899. Consecration of St. Mark's, Salisbury.

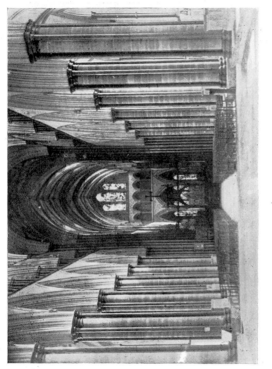

THE NAVE.

THE CHAPTER HOUSE.

The views in this volume are from the negatives of Mr. H. W. SALMON, Winchester; Mr. A. H. PITCHER, Gloucester; Mr. W. P. VARNEY, Lichfield, and Messrs. F. WETHERMAN & Co., Ltd., Enfield.

SOME BOOKS ❧ ❧
TO BE CONSULTED.

Introduction to Gothic Architecture. (Parker.)
  An invaluable book.
A.B.C. of Gothic Architecture. (Parker.)
A Concise Glossary of Architecture. (Parker.)
Murray's Handbooks to the Cathedrals.
  All later writers acknowledge obligation to Murray.
English Cathedrals Illustrated. F. Bond. (Newnes.)
  All the Cathedrals in one volume.
  A most interesting and well-illustrated book.
Cathedral Churches of England and Wales. Edited by Professor Bonney. 2 volumes. 12/- (Cassell.)
The "Builder" Portfolio of the Cathedrals.
  Of the greatest value.
History of Architecture. Fergusson. (Murray.)
